CREATIVE ACTING

CreativeSparksStudios Presents:

CREATIVE ACTING

The Trials & Tribulations
of a Working Actor

**Basic acting for anyone thinking
about acting, has acted,
think they can act,
or has said, "I can do that!"**

**This manual will show you how to act,
how not to act, basic acting techniques, how
to find an agent, the "business"
of acting, how to audition and
most important,
how to get out of your own way.**

Created by

Preston Sparks

a 30-year veteran of the acting profession.
CreativeSparksStudios.com

To order additional copies of this book, contact:
Xlibris Corporation
1-888-795-4274
www.Xlibris.com
Orders@Xlibris.com
50082

Contents

Thanks for the memories . . .

Very special thanks: To my lovely wife, Therese, my love and my dream come true. My sons: Jacob & Lucas who are my inspirations. My stepson & stepdaughter: Robert and Jacqueline, who are supportive of who I am.

Thanks to everyone that helped me with this book: Rose Marie Madsen, Niall Padden, Chris Hoag, Jason Lethcoe, David & Jeff, Scott Martin (who edit are of my mistakes so thoroughly), and to everyone who has taught me more then I could ever learn by myself.

Thanks to the Young Artists Ensemble
(*www.yaeonline.com*) for giving me the opportunity to
teach and learn.

I get by with the help of my friends.

Introduction

As an actor, always observe. Bare witness.

The Trials and Tribulations of a Working Actor!

I've been asked this question many times; "How did you get started as an actor and how do I get in the business?" That is an easy and also a hard question to answer. I can easily tell you how I got started but the answer to how you should get in the business varies, depending on whom you talk to. There are some in the business, or the fringes, who may think they have the answer about how to start an acting career. If anyone ever tells you they have the "best answer" and "guarantees you work," they don't know what they are talking about. No one, and I mean *no one,* can guarantee you work.

There are certain guidelines that will help and there are certain steps you should follow, but foremost, it is a hard and tedious road. I tell my students you just have to "PP" sometimes. What I mean by that is to be Patient and Persistence (PP). If you want to make a living acting, you need to be very patient, because chances are, it is going to take a long time. You also need to be persistent, because if you give up, you may never get another chance. I will share with you my own personal experiences and how I started my acting career.

I grew up in Baltimore, Maryland, and never considered acting. I was too busy just trying to survive. I did not do theater in high school but I did dabble in very small acting roles in college. I became President of the Student Body (Government) and did public speaking, which gave me some confidence being on stage. At 24 years of age, I heard the calling of, "Go west young man!"

So, I decided to go to California. I didn't go there to pursue acting or a modeling career, but to see what the West Coast was all about.

Shortly after arriving, getting a job and settling in, several people suggested that I give modeling or acting a try. I didn't believe I had the looks for modeling or the talent for acting, but eventually my curiosity (ego) took over. I decided to attend The American Academy of Dramatic Arts (AADA). I really enjoyed my acting experience at AADA and found out I did have a talent for acting. I decided to pursue an acting career, but easier said then done.

Being equipped with ignorance, arrogance and stupidity, off I went to seek fame and glory. The question I had to ask myself was: "Where do I start and how do I begin?" I began where most new talent starts, looking for opportunities, but none came. I did some local theater and developed some bad acting habits and went to look for a full-time job. I eventually worked at an engineering firm, which would allow me to come and go, as I needed to, they didn't know about it. I couldn't get a paying acting job no matter what I did, so I decided to settle into my job, pay some bills and pursue modeling. I attempted to get into several modeling agencies with no success. Finally a small agency took me, which had a modeling department as well as a commercial acting department. I did modeling for about a year and eventually the commercial department asked me to be a part of their agency. Let me think . . . ."Yeah!"

I went out on several auditions until I finally got my first commercial (whoopee). This commercial gave me the opportunity to join the Screen Actors Guild (SAG), which was my first step to becoming a "professional" actor, being paid for my acting. I did several more commercials after that and I decided to move to a bigger and better agency.

One thing you will learn is that you must treat acting like a business and do what is best for your career, even if that means moving around to different agencies.

I ended up at an agency that would allow me to audition for theatrical parts as well as commercials and modeling. I proceeded to make a living (on and off) for the next twenty years. Please note, in that 20 years, I had several different jobs to help support the acting career, everything from a waiter, roofer, handyman and almost anything I could do to survive. In those twenty years I worked on soap operas, did some films and television but my main source of income was from commercials. One thing you have to realize is that a career in the entertainment field is unpredictable and you *will* have your ups & downs.

While I was trying to make a living, I worked for an organization called the Young Artists Ensemble (YAE). YAE is a theater group, in Thousand Oaks, CA. The purpose of YAE is to give "kids" from 10 to 19 years of age, an opportunity to perform and understand all aspects of a theatrical production. When I was with YAE, I did scenic design/art, served as a technical director, built sets and also directed numerous productions. I began teaching acting classes for both kids and adults. I was motivated to teach acting because I would see many mistakes that were being made by the actors that could be resolved by proper techniques and an understanding of what "real acting" was. Through my teachings I discovered that many actors had misconceptions concerning a professional career in acting.

Most of the actors make basic assumptions about acting that are just not true: "It's easy!" "I could do that!" "I don't need training or experience!" "How hard could it be?" "My parents (family, friends) think I am "**good**" and should go professional." And many more misconceptions that in most cases lead to failure. These concepts lead to heartache and frustration. One of the biggest mistake actors make, is that they don't treat themselves like a product.

That may sound cold and impersonal but it is a reality.

You may be the cutest, the sexiest, the meanest, the most talented and the must **new & improved** star of this generation (or last), but if they (the business) can't market you and make money off of you, **they won't want you.** You also need to figure out the best way to present yourself and make yourself a "better product." Now, don't get me wrong, you have to believe in yourself and make yourself available to acting roles but you need to do it in a way that helps you get in the door and earn the job. You can do this by training, understanding the business, networking, knowing what kind of "product" you are and just plain luck, but you *must* have a plan, a commitment, a real perspective of what the business is about, and don't forget to be patient and persistent (PP).

Throughout this book I will attempt to give you practical information and an understanding of yourself and what is required of you to have a successful career in the multi-media industry.

Warning!

Acting may be dangerous to your health!

**Every time I meet someone I don't like I say:
"Have you ever thought of becoming an actor?"**

Warning!

Acting can cause the following side effects:
Anxiety, depression, over the counter drug abuse, illegal drug abuse, false friendships, divorce, self-destructive tendencies, alcoholism, extreme highs, extreme lows, suicide, wanting to quit but can't, and many more potentially life altering symptoms.

You have heard many times that acting is one of the hardest professions you can go into and that is because it is true. You must keep that in mind at all times. If you want to be a non-professional actor and just play, go for it. If you are serious about making acting a profession, don't forget that it is a *business.* No one has to like you or hire you if you are pretty and "special." They will only hire you if you have what they want and they think they can make money because of you. It does not matter what your age is, young or old, pretty or ugly, unique or extremely talented, they will only hire you if they think they can make money because of you. There is nothing better than working in a production, and nothing worse then when you are not working. We have all seen people on reality shows that have become "famous" because of their peculiar behaviors (i.e.; eating a bug). We have seen actors who do not any obvious talent, but become very successful. We have seen people who are incredibly talented but never get their *"big break."* The people who "love you" when you are famous, may not be there when you are not. I am not trying to depress you but to let you know that you must treat the acting profession like a *business.* Take the necessary steps if you want a professional career. That can be training, acting lessons, singing lessons and practical acting experience, among many other possibilities. Don't forget to read books, do networking, and prepare yourself. So if you get the opportunity to perform, you will be ready. There is an old definition of the word luck:

Luck is when opportunity meets preparation.

You must be prepared if the opportunity arrives because you may not get a second chance. Have a support system around you, a loving supportive family, friends, an education that you can pull upon and a way to make money to provide for yourself while you are not working.

Acting professionally takes hard work, dedication, preparation, luck, a "thick skin" plus a drive that can get you through the hard times. If you think you have all that, then this book can be your first step into the world of acting.

Special note: **Never,** and I mean **never** pay anyone money for the "opportunity" to act. There are "organizations" out there with the promise that they can make you a "star," a "model" and make you famous. No organization, agency, modeling school or acting school can promise you fame. If a "talent scout" approaches you and say you have that "extra special look", "talent" and "star quality" don't trust them. If you do decide to believe them, check them out thoroughly. Go to the better business bureau, call the local Screen Actors Guild office and check about their qualifications before you do anything. If they **truly think you are the next superstar**, then let them put *their* money where their mouths are. Trust me, if they think they can make money off you, they will.

Buyers beware!

What is Acting?

"Acting is not something someone wants to
do, it is something someone has to do."

What is Acting?

From Wikipedia, the free encyclopedia:

*Acting is the work of an **actor** or **actress**, which is a person in theatre, television, film, or any other storytelling medium who tells the story by portraying a character and, usually, speaking or singing the written text.*

From Merriam-Webster Dictionary:

Acting is the art or practice of representing a character on a stage or before cameras.

Needless to say there are many different definitions for acting. Some people look at acting as a place to play. As an opportunity to be "center stage." Others like the challenge to push themselves beyond what is comfortable. I personally feel that acting is a place to truly become someone else, to read and perform written text that you would never have the opportunity to do and experience what it would be like to be in a situation that is beyond your "normal" way of living. I have seen every level of actor, from the beginner to the true professional, and one thing they all have in common is the joy of portraying a story. You must do it for the joy of it, not because you want to be famous, not because you want love and acknowledgement, but because there is a passion inside that drives you to perform and to serve the story. Do it for the love of it, not because it will fill the emptiness inside. There are many successful actors who seek happiness and think by seeking fame and glory they will find it. They are usually disappointed and in some cases slowly self-destruct. Let acting be an extension of who you are, not just who you think it will make you.

You are unique and special—use it!

What kind of Actor are You?

Entertainer

Personality

True Actor

"Every snowflake is different, be yourself, don't end up melting with the rest of the flakes."

What Kind of Actor Are You?

There are three kinds of actors: the Entertainer, the Personality and the True Actor.

The Entertainer would be someone who is known for his or her entertaining personality and when you see him or her perform; you know it is going to be based on their personality. Jerry Seinfeld, Steve Carell, Will Ferrell, Adam Sandler, and Ellen Degeneres are a few examples of an entertainer actor.

The Entertainer develops their talents by creating a career for themselves and by establishing themselves as a comedian, singer/dancer, and an outrageous persona or as a unique personality. Their training usually is developed from stand-up, improvisation, TV, Community Theater, and through personal observations.

Personality actors would be individuals whose roles reflect their personal persona. Examples include: Arnold Schwarzenegger, Jessica Alba, Billy Crystal, Jim Carey, Drew Barrymore and Mike Myers. You never expect to see any of these actors in such acting roles as *Hamlet, Boys Don't Cry, Monster*, or any other dramatic or in some cases, comedic roles.

The Personality actor is usually created by the "stereotype" of their appearances, the acting roles that they were initially chosen for or their limited acting abilities. The audience will not usually accept this kind of actor in any other roles other than what they are known for. Examples of that would be Mike Myers in a serious dramatic role, Jim Carrey as Hamlet, Drew Barrymore as Queen Elizabeth or Arnold as the Pope.

The audience has a hard time accepting that these actors have the ability to perform these roles. Personality actors receive their training from many different classes, community theater, professional theater, television, movies; or they were thrust into a particular role by mere luck.

Actors who transform themselves with each role and become the character they are portraying would represent the **True Actor**. Sir Anthony Hopkins, Charlize Theron, Emma Thompson, Johnny Depp, Meryl Streep, Daniel Day-Lewis and Tom Hanks would be a few individuals that would represent a true actor. They allow the character to exist through them by meticulous research, understanding and surrendering to their characters. The great Stella Adler once said; "As the character, you must be willing to sh*t on stage." The meaning of this is that there are certain characteristics you as an individual would never do, but your character would.

To be a True Actor, you as an actor must surrender to what your character would do, not what you would do. Don't get me wrong; you should never do anything that would compromise your moral beliefs or the standard that you have set for yourself, be it personal or professional, but that is a decision you must make for yourself. There are some actors that will do anything for their character and others who would never comprise their values. The training that is involved in becoming a true actor can be very intensive and can take years to master. Then there are *actors who **don't** believe in training and "just go for it." I feel the actor who "goes for it" is doing a very hard technique to master and most actors cannot get out of their own way (surrender to their first impulses) to create such characters.

Each one of these categories is separate from the other, but each actor in each category can occasionally move from one to the next. It is more common for a true actor to move to the other categories then the other way around. The exception to that would be someone like Robin Williams who started out as an entertainer, became a personality and under the *proper director*, became a "true" actor.

All of these categories are important in their own right and are capable of providing for the actor and their families. The question you have to ask yourself is which category do you want to belong to? Every category has its place and requires hard work, dedication and a certain amount of luck. Dustin Hoffman and Meryl Streep take a methodical approach to their characters, break down every nuance, becomes the character by absorbing their lifestyles and eventually they cannot separate themselves from the character (method acting).

I have seen many students with intensive training not have the proper training to be successful in a professional environment. If you don't want to be a professional actor that's fine, but try to become the best actor you can be. I once had a student in my class who I was trying to give suggestions on how to improve a scene. He expressed to me, "I have done it this way in over a hundred plays!" I replied, "Well you have done it wrong a hundred times." Just because you have done it a certain way or have been taught a certain way,

---

*   In an interview, Tom Wilkinson believes it is just a matter of just reading the script, seeing the story in his mind and then surrendering to the character.

it doesn't mean it's right. It also doesn't mean it's wrong. It is up to you to go out and see different techniques to decide what is right for you and what is not. Don't forget you are interviewing the teacher, institution or theater, they are not interviewing you . . . make sure it is right for you.

The Different Styles of Acting

Theater

Television

Film

"I used to be different, but now I'm the same."

Different Styles of Acting

There are many different styles of acting, depending on the style in which you were trained. The style in which you were trained will reflect the way you present your acting. If you were theatrically trained, you will have tendencies to play to "the house" (theater) and may perform very broad (big). If you were film trained, you may act "small" or very much inward. Soap opera actors tend to be more dramatic, almost to the point of melodramatic. Commercially trained actors tend to keep it "light" and almost in a "selling" mode. I am not saying these actors cannot move from one category to the other but you must be aware of your particular style and play to the venue that you are performing or auditioning for.

I have taught theatrically trained actors, who audition for film and have played their characters too "big" and over the top. I have also seen film actors who have auditioned for theater that play it so "small" that you can't hear them in the back row. If you go into a film audition and play it broad (big), chances are you will be over the top and the casting director will not know if you can bring it in (small). The same thing is true for film actors. If you are auditioning for a play and you are in a 400-seat theater, it doesn't matter how "real" you are if the back row can't see or hear you. The way I like to direct is to start small and build for the house (set—stage) we are in. If the actor is aware of the "subtext"—the meaning under what is being said; then we can build the performance to fill the venue that we are performing for. In film, sometimes it just takes a look, an "inner feeling" or a small gesture or sound, which is enough to convey what is going on.

In theater, you need to be broader and sometimes communicate with a grand gesture, a "larger than normal look" or increased volume to address the back row, but *at all times*, it has to be real and heartfelt. Otherwise it will come across as patronizing or fake. If you are doing a melodrama, it should be broad at all times or how the director directs you.

The bottom line is that it must be real and heartfelt, no matter what the venue.

The Three Things You Should Know

"What you don't know can hurt you!"

The Three Things You Should Know

1. If you want a professional career in acting: marry rich or have an escape plan.

A lot of people think I am kidding when I say this, but I am not. I don't care who you are, being successful professionally or as an amateur, you are going to have downtime, time when you are not acting (working). You must have some kind of support system in place for these downtimes. Be it money stashed away, investments, a job that you can do on the side (bartender/waitress) or a partner that will help you in the times that you are not working. There is nothing sadder than to see someone with marketable talents that cannot pursue their dreams just because they have to pay their bills.

2. The most important person on stage (set) is the other person.

If you keep your focus on the other actor and the other actor does the same for you, you will have a compelling scene . . . I guarantee it. So many actors only worry about themselves and it is so self-indulgent that it takes away from the entire scene. In my acting class, I have, on occasion, shoved a partition between actors in my class because they were not interacting with each other. Keep your focus on the other actor and take your cues from them. I guarantee you, if you do this, not only will you look great, so will the other actor.

3. Never play to the audience, unless otherwise directed.

You will see actors playing to the audience and responding to the audience for a laugh or a dramatic pause. It is not uncommon for community theater actors to play to the audience. There are certain productions that require you to play to the audience; musicals, melodramas, narratives and many more different productions, but this is a decision that is made by the director, not the actor. Whenever you play to the audience, you are patronizing and the audience knows this, even on a sub-conscience level. You may give a good performance but you will probably never give a *great* performance.

The Four Basic Acting Steps

"Prepare yourself, then let it go!"

The Four Basic Acting Steps

1. **Read and Cold Read Well.** This may sound very basic, but it is not. You should be reading all the time. You never know when you are going to have to play a Doctor, Lawyer or Indian Chief. There are so many roles in which you, a man, will have to play a woman (Tootsie/Mrs. Doubtfire) or a woman who has to play a man (Victor-Victoria/Boys Don't Cry). With the realities of "green screen" there is ***no limit*** to who or what you may be performing opposite of. Not only do you have to be aware of what is "real" but you should be open to the possibilities of what is "not real." Let your imagination soar. You have to be informed about **everything** and well informed. With the Internet, books, movies, libraries, theater and television, you should be well educated for almost any role, be it history, different circumstances and situations.

   Learning to Cold Read. Cold reading is an art in itself. For almost every audition, the majority of us are going to have to cold read. If you can learn to cold read well, you will give a masterful performance. Cold reading is when someone, be it a casting director, director or someone in the production staff, hands you a scene (called sides) and asks you to read the sides with very little time to prepare. This can be very frightening to most actors. Sometimes you will be reading opposite another actor, but this is very rare. Most of the time you will be reading with an assistant, a member of the production team or in some cases, the casting director. A majority of the time these individuals are not actors or have read these scenes so many times before that they are just going through the motions.

   This can be very disconcerting and fear inducing for an actor who is untrained in cold reading techniques. Some actors cannot cold read well but are marvelous actors, but they will not be given the opportunity to show it because they did not get through the initial audition. Then there are some actors who can cold read well, but cannot go beyond that on the set (one note). The key is to be great at both.

   To do cold reading well you will need to learn the cold reading techniques. Cold reading is very simple, and only requires a simple technique that requires a lot of practice. The first mistake that actors make is, that they have their face in the script and read to the page, not to the other actor. The casting director does not care how well you read but how you react to the other actor. They know the script. Step one of cold reading is to get out of the page by doing the following: take a book, magazine, script (if you have one), anything that has the printed word on it and is in sentences. Take your finger and place it next to the first sentence and read the sentence out loud *above the page*, look down, get the next line and then do the same with the next sentence. Do this each day for as long as you can. **Practice! Practice! Practice!**

Initially, this is going to feel awkward and uncomfortable . . . that's the way it should feel. Do not say any of the sentences into the page, only above the page. You may only get one or two words out at a time, but after practicing, you soon will be able to read complete sentences above the page without it appearing that you are looking down. You are training your mind and eyes to pick up these sentences in a quick fashion. Don't forget the most important person **is the other person**. Keep your focus on them. In a very short period of time you will be reading as if you are not reading. Which brings us to the second step:

2. **Read, and look like you are having a conversation while you are reading.** This too is harder than it sounds. I am sure that everyone has heard someone reading from a book and in most cases it does not sound "normal". What I mean by "normal" is that it generally is louder or softer then their normal speaking voice. The cadences of the words are either rushed or too slow and they tend to be very nervous. Speaking in public is very hard to do. Some say that it is their number one fear. I know actors who would rather do an entire play than speak in public. If you can master conversation while reading you will be able to perform most television shows. Jerry Seinfield is not an actor, but an entertainer who has the ability to look like he is having a conversation while reading. His show "Seinfield" was based on conversations between four characters. "Everyone Loves Raymond" is based on that same format. Most soap operas are also people having conversations, some better then others. I have auditioned for shows in which I have "pushed" or "forced" dialogue and because of that, I didn't get the job. It is very hard to relax in a pressure situation, that's why it is important to practice your technique. Just read the copy (sides) and take your cue (reaction) from the other actor.

If you are truly having a conversation, you will truly react in the appropriate manner. I am sure that there have been moments in your life in which you have argued with someone, been in love with someone or even just had a conversation. You took your cues (reacted) from the other person. Do the same when you are reading a script. It doesn't mean you are not going to have feelings, but that brings us to step number 3.

3. **Inject emotions and feelings into your conversation.** This is where you start moving into "true acting". This requires **character development, subtext, choices, history of the character and what motivates the movement of the scene (what moves it forward).**

    Character development means to decide some important foundations of what makes the character (role) act the way they do. Where is your character from? What is your relationship to the other characters in the scene? What makes you, your character; act the way he or she does? Why are you there? What happened in the character's (your) childhood that would make them act this way? These are a few questions you need to ask about the character you are playing.

    Subtext is what is really being said underneath the dialogue. When you say something like "I love you!" that does not necessarily mean someone loves someone in the sense that they cannot live without him or her. What if they just had a fight and are angry with the other person? What if someone is leaving you and you don't want him or her to go? How many times in your life have you had to say "OK" but really were angry and did not want to say "OK"? That is subtext. There are many different meanings for every line . . . it is your job to determine what they are.

    Choices are what you work for in order to stimulate the emotional life in your character. The more choices you make, the richer and deeper your performance will be. Some of those choices would be: **Sensory Choice: see, feel, hear, smell and taste.**

    The Imaginary Monologue: Talking to people that have had an affect on your life, real or imaginary.

    Believability: By mixing truths with untruths, by saying things that aren't true until you believe them to be true.

History: Is when the time period or the character history affects the overall scene or the history between the characters. Your character will have some kind of "history" with other characters in the scene. Sometimes the history will be obvious, but not all the time. It is your job to determine what that history is and how you (the character) feel about others in the scenes. There are also certain elements today that would not be true in the 19th century or words or actions that would not be appropriate. You must at all times surrender to the character and the time period. Everyone has "history" between each other, even if you are only meeting the person for the first time. We make judgments based on what we think that person will be like because of experiences or prejudices we have had in the past. I personally feel that in a period film or play, no matter what the time period, *the real emotions* will be the same, be it the past, present or the future.

The next step is *moving the scene forward* or the *action* of the scene. Actions would include and not limited to the following: What do you, the character, want to do to the other person(s) (characters)? Do you, the character, want to kiss them, hit them, hug them, push them, fight, flee, hide or pinch their butt? The action is anything that keeps you focused on the other person or in the scene. These actions do not need to be communicated but felt, and *you determine* what action your character wants to do based on *character development, subtext, choices, and believability.*

Choices are anything in your life that affects you, (your character) whether they are positive or not. Use those choices to move or motivate the character forward.

4. **Instincts & Intuition:** This cannot be taught it just has to happen. This has happened to me a few times and it is an incredible feeling.

Great actors are "made" because of instinct & intuition. These actors are the ones that are comfortable enough in their own skin, acting abilities, trust themselves, done their homework and do not try to stop their characters. Hopefully when it does happen it is captured on film or is in front of a live audience. This does not mean you change the blocking or the lines and do something inappropriate or dangerous; just relax, don't think about it and trust your choices.

For example, when you are in a scene and you are truly reacting in character (did all of your character development) and out of nowhere, you do something or say something that is just incredible. And if you try to duplicate it, or **"try to make it happen"** again, you are going to fail.

One of the analogies I use is a sport analogy. When you are trying to hit a baseball, a tennis ball or even a golf ball, you need to practice, practice, practice to do it right. If you *think* about hitting the ball, chances are you are going to miss, slice (hit it to the left or right), "ground the ball" or many other possible combinations. The key with "hitting" the ball is to just relax and trust all of the practice you have done. The same is true with acting. Do all of the "practice" you can do, **make choices** and then just **relax and do it**. If you *try* to do it, chances are you are going to fail. Don't forget to be yourself and go for it.

Don't over think it-do it!

Additional Cold Reading Information

"Always, always, *listen!*"

Additional Cold Reading Information

When you first pick up the sides (script), only read it once, maybe twice at the most. I know for the majority of actors this is a very scary proposition. You will see many actors reading their sides over and over again and be busy "acting it out." What this does is make their performance look staged and predictable. By reading it over only once you will be more reactionary (react to what is going on) and your performance more unpredictable. If you learn the cold reading technique, keeping your eyes out of the page and make the other person more important than you, this will work.

This does not mean you don't make certain choices . . . you do. When you first read over the script, listen to your first impression of the scene. How do you see your character? Are they aggressive, passive, sad, horny, hurt, in love, happy or many other possible emotions? What do they want to do to the other character(s) in the scene? Do you want to hit the other characters in the scene, kiss them, move away from them, hug them, and pinch their bottom or many other ***actions?*** And what is your reaction to what they want to do? The bigger the action choice, the better; ***you do not communicate*** this to the interviewer or anyone else. These are your private choices and no one needs to know what they are. **There are no wrong choices.** If you go at it 110% the scene will be interesting and work. If they direct you to do it a different way, do it. This means they are interested in you and want to see if you can take direction and you have range.

Another thing you ***do not*** want to do in an interview is to take props in with you or wear a costume. I auditioned for a film where I had to kill a vampire. One of the other actors brought in wooden stakes and garlic, which was a joke and only made him look foolish. As far as costumes are concerned: don't wear anything that will distract from your performance. Do not dress in period pieces or elaborate articles. They have costume people and they do not need your input. This does not mean you don't dress appropriately. If you are reading for a businessperson, wear nice slacks and shirt or dress (if you are a woman). For a cowboy or construction worker, wear jeans and work shirt, don't wear the complete cowboy or construction worker gear unless instructed otherwise.

Don't worry about being nervous; you are supposed to be nervous. This is natural, just embrace it, and make it work for you. The few times I was *not* nervous, my scene was flat and not memorable. Just go with it, don't resist it.

Try to have fun and enjoy the opportunity to perform.

Commercials
Part I

Know what kind of product you are.
Be realistic!

Commercials: Part I

I have been very successful commercially. I have done more commercials than anything else (Theater, Television, Film) in my career. There was a time when so-called "serious" actors wouldn't do commercials because it was beneath them. That has changed. Today you can see all levels of actors doing commercials. There are actors who only do commercials, actors who have done commercials and then found themselves in a TV series and then you have actors that have been out of "the spotlight" for a period of time. They do a commercial to get back in the limelight and then end up with a series (Sally Field). You will also see established actors do commercials for the additional exposure or just for the money.

I have an actor friend who said that he does not do commercials because it isn't "real" acting. I told him to pretend that it was a part in a film and he had to act like he was in a commercial. Besides, I would rather do a commercial than wait on tables any day.

Commercials are very hard to do. It is very hard to be yourself, yet sell a product and make it look like you are not selling it, all in a few seconds. All you have to do is look at Union commercials versus non-union commercials. Union commercials have a nice easy flow to them, seem natural and sell the product. Non-union commercials in general, look forced (trying to hard), disjointed (all over the place) and silly. Don't get me wrong, they both serve a purpose in getting the message out, plus it is a great opportunity to make some money and practice your craft.

If you are not in the union (SAG) and you get the chance do some non-union commercials, do them . . . it will get you in front of the camera.

The good thing about commercials is that there is not a particular "type" for commercials. You can be short, tall, skinny, fat, good looking, ugly, a biker, a cowboy, a mom, sexy, a grandma or grandpa, almost anything you can think of, but there is one thing you have to be—marketable. You have to be something the client wants. The most important thing to remember is that the commercial is never about you; it is about the product. I have been the "hero" (the main character representing the product) in many commercials, the main character representing the product, but if I did not showcase the product, they would fire me.

Before we talk about how to act in a commercial, let me tell you how commercials are made.

The client, let's say Coca-Cola, decides they need a new commercial for their product. They go to their ad agency and tell them; "Make me a commercial!" The ad agency then presents their ideas to Coke, Coke picks one (maybe several), and off we go. The ad agency then calls a production house (generally in New York or LA) that has a director who specializes in commercials and has the production staff he needs. They then start breaking down the commercial by type, what kind of actors they need. Let's say they need an overweight guy (30's to 40's year of age), a skinny guy (same age), a housewife (25 to 35 year of age) and a dashing hero (30's). The production house then calls their casting service: a casting service is a business, which specializes in casting commercials or other productions. The production house then sends them (casting service) the "breakdowns" (breakdowns are what types they want to see). Then the casting house starts calling commercial agencies and tells them what type of actor they need to see.

Sometimes the casting service will ask for certain actors they know would be right for the part and also ask the commercial agencies to send others. Most of the time the casting service will only use the top agencies for their search, but will sometimes use smaller agencies.

The commercial agency will start pulling pictures of their clients that would be right for the part, and send the pictures over to the casting service. More often than not, "pictures" are sent via the computer. The casting director then decides whom they would like to see, calls the commercial agencies and tell them whom they would like to see and also gives the commercial agency the time & place. The agency calls their clients (actors) that they feel are right for this commercial. The actors get the time, place, product, what they should wear and told if there is dialogue or not. If there is dialogue, the actor can generally get it from a casting service or they will try to get to the interview early to go over the copy (sides).

When the actor arrives, he or she will be in a room with many other actors that fit "the type" that the casting service wants to see. The actor then will sign-in on a audition sheet and be called either by your appointment time or when you arrived. You will go into a room with a camera operator (generally an actor), act out the scene and if there is any dialogue you will also do that. You will say "Thank You!" to the camera operator, drive home and think of how you should of have done it better, wait by your phone and hopefully get a callback.

After everyone has been seen, the casting director will send the tape or DVD to the production house where a representative from the client (Coca-Cola), the ad agency and director will look at the auditions. They will decide whom they want to see on the callbacks and send it off to the casting service.

The casting service will get in touch with the commercial agencies that have the actors they want to see and request them at the callback. The agencies call the actors and give them the date, time and place of the callbacks. The actors then go to the callback, they are happy now because they got a callback, and then they will audition again.

This time there will be fewer actors, because the only ones that will be there will be the actors that got a callback. You will sign in again, wait your turn, and then be called into the audition room. This time, however, in the room will be the client (Coca-Cola), the ad agency, the director and several people I have no idea why they are there and of course, the camera operator. You'll do the scene again and then everyone gets to critique your performance. Chances are, the director will give you direction on what he wants, and you'll do it again and then be finished. You will say "Thank you!" If you try to say something clever, it will fail, and then you'll take the long drive home and sit by your telephone. If you get the job (yeah!) your agent will call you, and you will be excited and say they will be back in touch with you about, wardrobe, the time and place.

Doesn't that sound glamorous?

Commercials
Part II

Be the "New & Approved" you.
Always find ways to get better.

Commercials: Part II

The keys to working are three fold:

1. Get a good agent.
2. Know what "type" you are.
3. Know how to properly act (perform) in commercials.

1. If you want to get a good agent, someone who has an "in" with casting services, it is very hard to do. You must actually have worked to get a good agent and you can't work unless you have a good agent. OUCH! The old catch 22. To add to the difficulties, if you are not in the Screen Actors Guild (SAG) it makes it even harder to get one of the top agents. Unless you have a unique look (three eyes) or talent, most agents will not take you as a new client. Whenever possible you can try to do non-union (not recognized by SAG) work, but try not to develop bad working habits.

Some casting services offer commercial workshops (acting classes) and I suggest if you can, take one of them. This will give you professional commercial acting experience and an "in" with that casting service. Make sure that they are a **real** commercial casting service and an agency that specializes in casting union commercials. There are some schools out there that will say that they can train you and get you work, but **no one** can guarantee you that. You can go to smaller agencies and hope they have enough clout to get you into some professional auditions.

The way I got into the union (SAG) and commercials was I started as a model in a smaller agency that had a commercial department. Eventually the commercial department wanted me and sent me on auditions, finally got my first commercial job and signed a *Taft-Hartley contract

---

* Taft-Hartley: The practice of allowing non-union actors to work on a union project provided that the actor subsequently joins the union as stipulated by certain provision of the Taft-Hartley Act. Generally this is only done if the actor has a unique look or some special qualification.

to get in the union. Once I did several commercials, I then signed with a bigger agency. I know it seems unfair to leave the agency that got me established but actors move around all the time. Agencies would let you go if you didn't work and don't forget, *it is a business!* If you don't get the opportunity to "get in the door," then do the old standby of mailing out your picture, a cover letter, a resume and hope for the best.

2. Knowing what type you are: this is harder then it sounds. You have to remember that you are a *"PRODUCT!"*, a unique product, but a product just the same. You are going to be judged on your appearance, it will be a lot easier if you just surrender to that until you can prove otherwise. If you are short, chances are you're not going to be cast as a basketball player. If you're tall, you won't get a chance to be one of the munchkins in a Wizard of Oz type commercial. If you are pretty, you probably won't be cast as someone ugly or visa-versa. You need to know your type. In commercials, they do not have any trouble finding the "right type."

    Look at yourself as a product, be honest about it and make *who you really are* something special and unique, because you are.

3. *Acting in television commercials* is harder than it looks. Almost everyone thinks, **"they could do that"** or, **"it's easy."** These are people who have never done a commercial. Until you have had a camera three inches from your face and are told to just **"be natural,"** you don't realize how difficult it is. Commercials are very competitive and you are constantly under pressure to "be real and yourself" this includes when you are supposed to pretend to be in Hawaii, in swim trunks, in the ocean that is 58 degrees and don't forget to **Smile!** The most important and hardest part about commercials is that you have to be yourself and *just relax.* They (the director) can read whatever is going on with you in a heartbeat. They can see it in your eyes and body. You can't fake it, you have to be in the moment and feel it.

The same four steps that I gave you for other acting are also true for commercials.

1. Read and cold read well.
2. Look like you are having conversation while reading.
3. Inject feelings and emotions into what you are reading.
4. Trust your instincts and intuition.

Commercials are instant. It has to be communicated in seconds. There is no time to build a character . . . you need to be yourself as the character.

The camera operator will direct you as to what the director and client want: listen and do.

There are three things to remember:

1. The product is the center of attention.
2. If there are other actors in the commercials react to them honestly. Don't upstage them; it will only make you look bad.
3. If you are talking to the camera, treat it as if it is real and if possible, a person you know.

Try not to use "*your announcer voice*" (unless directed otherwise) and just keep it conversational and real. The best thing to do in a commercial audition is to be relaxed and be you, easier said then done. When you are finished, thank the camera operator; they can be your best friend or your worst enemy; do you like to be in focus? Leave the audition and try not to think of the commercial until you get a callback. Commercial auditions can play with your mind, be very frustrating and they can make you depressed. They can also be a great source of income and give you the opportunity to work (act) under pressure. The main thing is, don't give up! Enjoy the fact that you are auditioning and enjoy the process.

Relax, be yourself, have fun and don't forget to breathe.

Good is Bad

**"If all of your friends are losers, then
you should look at yourself."**

Good is Bad

There is nothing worse than a "good" actor. Good is predicable and boring. There are so many good actors around the world, and being a *good actor* will not make you stand out. Somewhere right now in the world, in the United States, colleges, high schools or down the street, someone is telling someone, "You are good and should go to Hollywood or New York!" YIPES! Actors come from all around the world, be it by plane, train, or automobile to get into the "business." There are good actors in New York, Hollywood and every major city in the world and the *good* actors just get lost in the shuffle.

We have heard singers on reality shows that are "good," but unless they have that *extra something special,* they will end up singing in some small nightclub or not at all. I am not saying this is all bad, but unless you have that extra special something that makes you standout or by shear luck, the chances of making it is slim. I do not want to discourage you, but want to make you realize that you need to put in that extra effort and develop your craft. I know you have heard how hard it is to get into the business and the rejection that actors constantly face. **This is because it is true.** I know you have heard of actors that were "discovered", and were overnight successes, you heard about it because it is the exception to the rule and not normal. Even with the actors that were "discovered," they probably put in a lot of groundwork and had been trying for years to get "discovered."

You have to get out of "good" and become something unique and different and *just be who you are!*

That doesn't mean you shouldn't work on technique or the foundation of your craft but to use that to promote your own special qualities.

Some of my favorite actors are first time students. Their performances are unpredictable and focused. They have not learned any **"tricks"**! What I mean by tricks is when an actor gives that "predictable look," that "hand gesture," a certain "inflection" of a word and many other tricks that actors have learned from bad teachers or community theater. The first time actor, is generally being genuine and just being themselves in the situation, and it is refreshing and fun to watch. The hardest thing for an actor to do is to get rid of their tricks. It is a safe place for an actor, but an experienced casting director or commercial director will see your tricks right away and will say, "Thank you very much". Which means, I will never see you again. I would rather see someone who is "bad" and gives me a true glimpse of themselves and who *they really are,* than an actor who is good with tricks. There is nothing wrong with tricks in a non-professional arena, but the majority of the time, when you bring them into a professional audition, they will appear amateurish and the director will see right through them.

Be true to yourself and the material. Take a chance. Make it happen. Make choices. Take action. Don't forget the basics, cold read well, have conversation while reading, inject emotions and feelings into the conversation and let your instincts and intuition take over.

Trust and believe in who you are and use who you are!

Free Acting Classes

"Swing the bat, but know how: practice!"

Free Acting Classes

There are many free acting classes. One of the best free class is to just audition whenever you get the chance. Pick up your local trade publication for your area, be it theater, local student films or independent films and then audition. Practice your cold reading technique and practice under pressure. You do not have to take any acting job that is offered to you but it will give you enough practical knowledge so if a "real" acting job comes along, you will be more prepared. If you are not in the unions: SAG, AFTRA, AEA or others, this is a great opportunity to do non-union work.

Once you are in the unions, there are many restrictions to doing non-union work. Check with your union. Also check with your local colleges and see if they have a film department or theater department and try to audition or even act in some of their productions. You can also audition for local community theater productions, but be aware; there are some productions (theater, film, schools) that can get you into some bad working habits. **Be Careful!**

You can always take acting classes, which can cost very little or a lot, but some acting classes are good and some are not. Remember, ***You should interview them,*** and don't worry if they will "let you know" if you got "in" or not. If your check clears, the majority of these schools will say, "You are qualified." Look at the students in the class, are they aspiring actors, housewives or just looking for something to do? I have taught several classes with all of the above and many of my students have gone off and perused professional careers. If you don't like the teacher, then don't take the class. Your relationship with the teacher should be a safe haven and they should be tough but also supportive. Acting classes are a place where you should be completely vulnerable and willing to take chances, and it needs to be a secure environment.

A great way to practice without paying for classes is to put your television on "closed caption" and read the dialogue being broadcasted out loud. This is especially good for getting the flow of the dialogue and the tempo of the written word. If you do this for commercials, you will quickly discover *how easy* and yet *how hard* the dialogue actually is. Anytime you get an opportunity to read out loud, do it. Be the one who wants to give that speech, raises their hand and addresses the crowds. It doesn't mean you won't be nervous, but it will give you an opportunity to work on controlling your nerves and fears and doing it anyhow.

Be creative! Try to find that opportunity to be the center of attention. Everyone that knows me well will tell you that I try to do that all the time, sometimes too much.

William Shakespeare said:
"The world is just a stage where men and women are merely players."
Play!

The ABC's of Casting—Literally!

What letter are you?

The ABC's of Casting-Literally

All productions, be film, television or theaters have an ABC of casting. You have probably heard of "A" actors, "B" actors, "C" actors and "Kathy Griffin's on the D list." That is because there is an alphabetical rating for actors.

Let me give you a breakdown of the list.

The "A" List: Actors you want but probably would not do the role if offered.

The "B" List: Actors who will do the role if the production can afford them.

The "C" List: Actors you can afford and probably do the role.

The "D" List: Actors you should see for the role.

The "E" List: Actors or agents that you owe favors to and you should see their actor for the role.

The "F" List: Actors that are submitted by agents for the role that would be good for the role and you should see.

The "G" List: Actors that the casting director, director or producer owes a favor too.

The "H" List: Known actors that submit themselves for the role.

The "I" List: Actors that are seen in other productions that you should consider.

The "J" List: Unknown actors that submit themselves.

The "K" List: Actors that "network", hoping to be discovered.

The "L" List: The thousand of actors that are in the unions that hope they get a lucky break.

The "M" List: The thousand of actors that aren't in any unions that wishes and prays for any role.

The "N" List: Actors that are "good" and are sitting at home, hoping that a miracle will happen: That the "Acting Angel" will come out of the sky and fly them off to Hollywood (or New York)! Good luck with that!

And the beat goes on and on. Where do you fall on the list?

The Unions

United we stand. If you want to do it alone,
that's what you will be, alone.

Unions: To Join or Not to Join:
That is the Question?

If you want to be a professional actor, eventually you will have to join a union. Unions are there to protect you. They were created to keep production companies, agents and other entities of the business from taking advantage of you. They provide work standards from the minimum you can get paid, to providing you with benefits like health insurance, pensions, scheduled breaks and a place to go if you need help or support and many more outstanding benefits.

There was a short period in my career where I was having a hard time financially and with health, and the SAG Foundation came to my rescue. I will always be grateful for their support and understanding.

There are three main unions that you will need to join in order to work professionally. Those unions are the Screen Actors Guild (SAG), the American Federation of Television and Radio Artists (AFTRA) and the Actor's Equity Association (AEA).

SAG represents actors who work in motion pictures, television, commercials, industrials, video games, Internet and all new media. Once you become a SAG member one of the requirements is that you make sure that any project you work on is recognized by SAG. To get into SAG is harder then most unions. The requirements for joining are located under "SAG" in the upcoming pages.

AFTRA represents professional actors, dancers, singers and broadcasters. AFTRA is geared toward "three camera shoots", such as soap operas, sitcoms, news broadcasters and other performers with video type shoots. The requirements for joining are also listed in the upcoming pages.

AEA represents Actors and Stage Managers in the United States. There are different unions in other countries. If you work on the stage professionally and get paid, as an actor or a stage manager, you will eventually need to join the AEA.

Unions are necessary for having a protected and long career but non-union work is an opportunity for you to get in some work and to practice your craft. Just remember that your work conditions will not be protected and you can easily be taken advantage of. There are productions that will give you an opportunity to work (act) but you may have to contribute to the production, be it you give them money or helping out on the set. My rule of thumb is that I will work for free but I will not pay for the opportunity to perform.

I don't mind helping out a production if I can, but only to a certain extent. This is a personal choice you will have to make. When you go to auditions, make sure you take someone with you; especially if it is an area you don't know or is remote. If someone suggests that you remove your clothes, don't do it unless you are comfortable with it and the part truly requires it. This suggestion should never be made on the first audition and only when the production has narrowed it down to a few actors. If you are under 18, never do it, and no matter what your age, you can request that someone be in the room with you.

This rule also goes for photographs. Even if the photograph is going to be "artsy", I suggest you don't do it and whatever you do, don't sign a models release form. You never know where or when these photos or film may appear.

Audition or perform in local theater productions, your local colleges and film schools in your area. If you just want to play, remain an amateur, it is okay not to join a union, but if you want a career, then you will eventually have to join a union.

I do not teach in my acting classes with the intention of making someone a professional actor, but to give them skills that they can use throughout their lives. If you can speak in public, read intelligently, and are able to be a team player, I have done my job. If you do work professionally, than that is just the icing on the cake.

Screen Actors Guild—SAG

Screen Actors Guild (better known as SAG) members are actors who work in motion pictures, television, commercials, industrials, video games, Internet and all new media formats. SAG is a hard union to get into. You need to work in a union production to get into SAG, but you can't work on a union production unless you are in the union. (?) But there are some special exceptions to qualify.

Steps to join SAG: How do you qualify?

A performer becomes eligible for Screen Actors Guild membership under one of the following two conditions:

1. Proof of SAG employment
2. Employment under an affiliated performer's union

Proof of Employment:

Principal Performer Employment:

Performers may join SAG upon proof of employment.

Employment must be in a principal or speaking role in a SAG film, videotape, television program or commercial. Proof of such employment may be in the form of a signed contract, or original pay stub(s). The document proving employment must provide the following:

❖ Applicant's name
❖ Applicant's Social Security number
❖ Name of the production or name of the commercial (product name)
❖ The salary paid (in dollar amounts) and,
❖ The specific dates worked

Background Actors (Extras) may join SAG upon proof of employment as a SAG-covered background player at full SAG rates and conditions for a *minimum* of three working days subsequent to March 25th, 1990. Employment must be by a company signed to a SAG Agreement under which the producer is required to cover background actors. Proof of employment must be in the form of original pay stubs or a payroll printout faxed from the payroll house. Such documents must be provided the same information (name, Social Security number, etc.) as listed above.

Employment under an affiliated performer's union:

Performers may join SAG if the applicant is a paid-up member of an affiliated performers union (ACTRA, AEA, AFTRA, AGMA or AGVA) for a period of one year and has worked and been paid for at least once as a principal performer in that union's jurisdiction.

This information and more can be found on the SAG's website which is: *www.sag.org*. If you have specific questions you can call: 323-954-1600 (Hollywood), 212-944-1030 (New York) or check with your local SAG office.

(Taken from the SAG website: *www.sag.org* as of January 2008)

American Federation of Television & Radio Artists (AFTRA)

AFTRA represents professional actors, dancers, singers and broadcasters.

It is simple to join AFTRA. You need to pay a one-time initiation fee and dues for the current dues period.

Professional performers or broadcasters who wish to join AFTRA should contact their local AFTRA office or the national membership department at (866) 855-5191 or e-mail to: *membership@aftra.com* to find out more about AFTRA, the services it provides and how to join.

(Information taken from *www.aftra.org* website as of January, 2008)

Actors Equity Association—AEA

AEA represents more than 45,000 actors and stage managers in the United States.

Overview to join:

> The Equity Membership Candidate Program (EMC) permits actors and stage managers in training to credit theatrical work in certain Equity theaters towards eventual membership in Equity. Candidates must complete 50 creditable weeks of work at any of the participating theaters. The weeks do not have to be consecutive and may be accumulated over any length of time.

If you have additional questions go to the Actors Equity Association website at *www.actorsequity.org* or call National headquarters in New York at 212-869-8530 or Western Region Headquarters in Los Angeles at 323-634-1750.

(Information taken from Actors Equity Website *www.actorsequity.org* as of: January 2008)

Contact Information for Unions

Screen Actors Guild
(SAG)
www.sag.org
Hollywood, CA 323-954-1600

American Federation of Television & Radio Artists (AFTRA)
www.aftra.org
866-855-5191

Actors Equity Association
(AEA)
www.actorsequity.org
New York, NY 212-869-8530
Los Angeles, CA 323-634-1750

Alliance of Canadian Cinema, Television & Radio Assoc.
(ACTRA)
www.actra.ca
800-387-3516

American Guild of Musical Artists
(AGMA)
www.musicalartists.org
New York, NY 212-265-3687

American Guild of Variety Artists
(AGVA)
www.varietyartists.org
New York, NY 212-265-3687

Agents and Managers

Don't be cocky—be confident! The difference between
cocky and confident is, cocky people will let you
how great they are, confident people know they are
great and don't have the need to say anything!

Agents & Managers

Agents

There are several clichés concerning agents; "You're only as good as your agent", and "I can't get work without an agent, but I can't get an agent unless I work!" The reason these cliché exist is because there are true. You are only as good as your agent. If you have one of the top agents, you will be able to go out for the best projects. If you are not working, the agency doesn't need you, but they will want you if you are working. That's why it is hard to get a good agent. If you are not making money, they are not making money. All agencies work on commission, which is generally 10% of your earnings.

You should *never* pay someone or an agency to represent you. If they tell you that you need to pay a "processing fee", "a monthly fee" (dues), or any type of "fees" for them to represent you, move on—run! *No* legitimate agency will ask for money . . . they don't need it. If any agency offers acting classes or has a "friend" that is a photographer, *do not* sign with them. Agencies are in the business to get you work, not to offer you acting classes or photographers. A legitimate agency may offer you a list of photographers or classes that you *could* see, but they should not recommend them.

It is up to you to interview photographers and to audit acting classes. Screen Actors Guild (SAG), the American Federation of Television & Radio Association (AFTRA) or the Actors Equity Association (AEA) will usually franchise legitimate agencies. As your career becomes bigger and more prestigious, so should your agency, because your agency should reflect your position in the theatrical industry.

Managers

Let me say right up front, I have a bias against managers. Managers do not have to be licensed or recognized by any of the unions and anyone can become a manager. Don't get me wrong; managers are necessary for established actors. Managers can help them chose the right paths for their careers, but you do not need a manager unless you have something to manage. Managers will ask for 15% of your earnings and will not necessary get you work. There are some managers who will sign you to a contract, hope you get a good agent, get work and because you are under contract with them, they will take 15% of your earnings, even if they do nothing. Yes I know, you are special, unique and different from everyone else, but wait until you become that superstar before you get a manager.

Special note: If you ever think about signing with an agent or even a manager, do your homework first, check them out, and see if they are on the Internet. If possible, talk to some of their clients. Ask the clients if they are working, how long they have been with a particular agent or manager (yuck!); what are their opinions of the agency and would they sign with that agency again. You can call the unions (SAG, AFTRA, etc.) and see if there are any reports concerning a manager or agency, good or bad. I know when you are first starting out you are thrilled that someone takes an interest in you, but that doesn't mean you should give up your rights or go down a path that is destructive to your career.

The best way to get an agent is to go to SAG's website (*www.sag.org*), get a list of recognized agencies, send out a cover letter, attach a photo (see photo chapter), include a resume (be honest) and hope for the best.

Photographs and Resumes

**The camera will always tell the truth,
so should your resume.**

Photographs

Photographs are an important part of your acting career and should be taken seriously. If you are an amateur and want to remain that way, a simple photograph is more than enough. If you want a career as a professional actor, your photo is your calling card and sometimes your first introduction to a casting director, agent or someone in the business. Make sure the photos represent whom *you truly are.* I know we all would like to see ourselves as that "superhero", that "sex kitten", the "rough and rugged cowboy" or the way we would like others to perceive us, but you need to actually look the way you are. Not with two tons of make-up, weird costumes, or in front of elaborate backgrounds, but the way you actually look.

If you dress up like a cowboy/girl or a hooker, that is all you are going to be called in for, if that is what you want, then go for it. If you want to be called in for as many roles as possible, try to make your look more generic, more non-descript, just a reflection of who you are. Any *good* agent, casting director or director will have the ability to see you in many different roles. Make sure they represent whom you truly are.

There was a time when the only thing casting directors and agents wanted was an 8x10 black & white headshot, but that has changed. Now they want to see photographs in color. Casting used to be done "face to face" or on "go sees" and had a more intimate feel, but now almost all casting is done via the Internet.

Your photos will be posted not only on your agents website, but also though casting services, such-as,

LA Casting (*www.lacasting.com*) or Casting Network (*www.castingnetworks. com*). There is a charge to be on these websites, but it is necessary and worth it. That is why it is so important to pick a great photo and a great photographer.

If you are anywhere near LA or NY, there are hundreds of photographers to chose from. You can afford to be picky and take your time. There are a few things you should keep in mind when picking a good photographer. If you are trying to go professional, *do not* use family, friends, wedding photographers or just anyone claiming to be a photographer. The photographer should have a professional portfolio. This portfolio should be with pictures representing what you want and not "artsy" photos of nudes, dogs, flowers or sunsets. These photos are great if you want to hang them in your house but not great if you are trying to start a career. You can go on-line and get real examples of professional headshots. You do not need to go overboard with pictures, just try to get enough photos to represent your look.

Here are tips you should look for in your own photos:

1. Keep them simple. Don't over complicate them with elaborate backgrounds or being overdressed.
2. If you are the "All American Type" portray that by having a simple outfit on, not something that takes away from you.
3. Look directly at the camera, not off in the sunset watching the dolphins play. Smile! Be warm and inviting.
4. Try to just be yourself in several different outfits.
5. If you are a character type (cowboy, biker, stripper) and that's all you want to be: portray that as real as possible.
6. Commercial headshots and theatrical headshots will have slight differences. Commercial headshots will be friendlier and generally look like you are approachable. Theatrical headshots tend to be more focused and direct, but this depends on what you are going for. If you feel that you can only play the "heavy" or the "temptress" then gear the photos in that direction.
7. Don't over-complicate pictures by putting a lot in the background or wearing outrageous costumes. This will only distract from you.
8. *Do not* do nudes or sexually suggested photos, unless that is a direction you want to go in. If the photographer says that this is for his "private collection" and "no one will see them", don't do them unless you want them to be posted on the Internet. Also, you'll never know, but one day when you are a superstar, I guarantee you, they will reappear.
9. There are photographers who will exploit you. If at anytime you feel uncomfortable, leave and demand your money back.

10. Whether male or female, you should always take someone with you on a photo shoot. That way you will always have support and backup in case something goes wrong. I know I am being a little paranoid here, but better safe then sorry.

A photo is something you will want to show for a lifetime, not something you'll keep secret.

Picking a Photographer

When you are ready to chose a photographer, *remember, you are interviewing them, they are not interviewing you!* Anytime you give money to someone, you are hiring them, which includes agents (that is why they call us clients). When you are looking for a photographer, you should interview at least three. Look at their portfolios and see if you like what you see. Talk price and find out what you can get for your money. Do you get the complete DVD's of the pictures? If they shoot with negatives, do you get the negatives back? Do they have a re-shoot policy? Do they shoot inside (studio) or outside? And most important, do *you* like them? If you don't, then don't work with them. Your photos will reflect your feelings and you will look forced (not natural) and uncomfortable. The photographer is not doing you a favor by taking your pictures (and money). If anything, you are allowing them to have a major part in your career and your relationship needs to be an equal partnership.

When the photo shoot is over and you get your DVD, negatives and/or proofs, take them to your agent (if you have one) and let them help you pick out the best photos for you. If you don't have an agent, be careful who you let decide which photos are "best." It is very hard for you, family and friends to be objective. They tend to see the person they know and not a professional actor. An acting teacher, a friend (who is in the business), or the photographer will be more objective and should know what is required.

When you finally pick out those winning photos, you generally only need two or three photos at the most. Take your DVD or negatives to a professional printing house that specializes in actor's headshots and get some copies made. You don't need "glossies" any more and lithographs are more then adequate. There was a time when you needed hundreds of copies, that is not true anymore. With the Internet and the creation of Internet casting services, you only need about 50 copies of each photo that you decided on. These photos will be used to mail for submissions and to hand out to agents, casting directors and people in the business. I had business cards made with my picture, cell phone number and e-mail address on them. When I am out and I meet someone that is in the business, I hand these out. It's not as pretentious as trying to hand an 8x10.

You should take new photos every couple of years, five years at the most, but if your look changes or you are young, you should probably do it every year or so.

The most important thing to remember is that your photos are a reflection of *who you really are!* The last thing you want to happen is when you go into an interview and have them ask, **"Is this you?"**

Keep it real, keep it honest, keep it simple and believe in yourself!

SMILE!

Preston Sparks

Resumes

Resumes are the second half of your calling card, your photo being your first, and should reflect your experience and your talents. With the Internet and our ability to find out almost anything about anybody, **you need to be honest!** I know you probably don't have a lot of experience, but that is okay. No one expects you to have a lot of experience, if you are just starting out. They are just looking for your look and want you, to be you. There was a time when actors would "pack" their resumes, fill it with lies, those days are over. It is just better to tell the truth. It will not affect your chances if they want to see you. Your talent and look will determine if you are right for their agency or for that part.

(A sample resume is on the following page)

Name Here

Cell: Number
E-mail Address

Height: **Hair:** (color)
Weight: **Eyes:** (color)

Agent's Name (if you have one)
Agent's phone number

Television:
*The Young & the Restless   Recurring   CBS (or director)
(Continue putting down experience in order (by date) any work you may have—if you don't have any, move to next category.)

Film:
*Wild, Wild West   Co-staring   Warner Bros. (or director)
(Continue putting down experience in order (by date) any work you may have—if you don't have any, move to next category.)

Theater:
*The Three Musketeers   Aramis   Gothic Production
(Continue putting down experience in order (by date) any work you may have—if you don't have any, move to next category.)

Training:
Preston Sparks Acting Workshops
The American Academy of Dramatic Arts
(Continue putting down experience in order (by date) any work you may have—if you don't have any, move to next category.)

Abilities:
Equestrian, karate (Black Belt-Shotokan), roller skating, smiling, leap tall buildings in a single bound . . . etc,

Commercials Upon Request

Please note: this is a sample template and you may adjust anyway you feel that works best for you. This resume should be attached or printed on the back of your photograph on an 8x10 format. If you don't have any experience or training, just put down you have a charming personality and are looking for work. *If you have worked a lot, only put down your must recent work.

Conclusion

(The Final Curtain)

"There is never an ending, just new beginnings."

Conclusion

I hope I have given you useful information about the acting industry. If you decide that you want to pursue acting as a professional actor, then you must realize that it is a business and not something you pursue lightly. There is nothing wrong with treating acting as a hobby or something you do for pleasure and enjoying acting in a leisurely way. But never think, as a career, that it is going to be easy to master. There are *many* talented actors who did not get their career off the ground because they thought acting was easy and that they were the *exception* to the rule. *The rules* are the same for everyone, even the ones *"who make it."*

The "ones that make it" can find themselves in a self-destructive free-fall and cannot stop it if they are not properly prepared. They didn't prepare for the *ups and downs* of the business. It is not only important financially but also emotionally. No one has to hire you because you are cute, sexy, funny, been trained at the *"best schools"* or are *"special."* They will only hire you if you are what they want and you can deliver what they need, money. You have to think of yourself as a product . . . unique, but a product just the same. You have to believe in yourself and don't act like someone else. **Just be you!**

If you wanted to become a professional baseball player, an accountant, a singer, a dancer or almost any other occupation, you would take classes, practice, go to schools or have private coaches. You would do whatever you could to become better in your chosen field of expertise. **Don't sit back and wait "to be discovered," go out and make it happen!** Have a plan, have a way to create an income, have a support system and work on your craft.

If you don't get a particular job or you fail in an audition, it doesn't mean it is over. When a batter strikes out, he doesn't go home and refuse to bat again, he tries to figure out what went wrong, and he practices and tries again. Some of the best homerun hitters are also the leaders in strikeouts. The same is true in acting. I have been rejected so many times I can't even tell you how many, but I continue to put it out there and I prepare for the best (and the worst). *You will be rejected* many times before you hit your first "homerun," If you can't handle rejection; you are in the wrong business. You *have to believe in yourself.* If you don't believe in yourself, don't expect others to. Be confident, not full of yourself (cocky). Be prepared. Have the support system you need: family and friends, a way to make income when you are not working, a training program and a true perspective of what the business is really about.

The hardest thing to do is to relax, trust yourself and your craft. If you put in the hard work, the practice and the effort, it will become easier and easier, the opportunities will happen.

Smile, relax, breathe and pursue acting with the respect it deserves. Let this be your first steps in your long and fruitful career as an actor.

www.ingramcontent.com/pod-product-compliance
Lightning Source LLC
Chambersburg PA
CBHW031325290526
45784CB00014B/2211